# DRONES

SCIENCE · TECHNOLOGY · ENGINEERING

BY STEVEN OTFINOSKI

CHILDREN'S PRESS®

An Imprint of Scholastic Inc.

CONTENT CONSULTANT

Matthew Lammi, Assistant Professor of Technology, Engineering & Design Education, North Carolina State University

PHOTOGRAPHS ©: cover: Chine Nouvelle/SIPA/Newscom; 3: Alexander Kesselaar/EyeEm/Getty Images; 4 left: AP Images; 4 right: Alexander Kesselaar/EyeEm/Getty Images; 5 left: Bloomberg/Getty Images; 5 right: J.W.Alker/imageBROKER/Superstock, Inc.; 6: Mc Antonio P. Turretto/ZUMA Press/Newscom; 8: Science Source; 9: Boyer/Getty Images; 10 left: Buyenlarge/Getty Images; 10 right: Sojka Libor/AP Images; 11 top: Zenith Electronics Corp./KRT/Newscom; 11 bottom: Desiga/Dreamstime; 12: AP Images; 13: Keystone/Getty Images; 14 left: Claudio Divizia/Thinkstock; 14 right: AP Images; 15 top: Everett Collection Historical/Alamy Images; 15 bottom: Henri Huet/AP Images; 16: Petty Officer 3rd Class Jeffrey S. Viano/U.S. Navy/Getty Images; 17: Anja Niedringhaus/AP Images; 18: Alexander Kesselaar/EyeEm/Getty Images; 20: Dale G. Young/AP Images; 21: -/AFP/Getty Images; 22: Marek Uliasz/Dreamstime; 23: ZUMA Press, Inc/Alamy Images; 24 top: Mechanik/Dreamstime; 24 bottom: dpa picture alliance/Alamy Images; 25: David Forster/Alamy Images; 26: USGS; 27: Mariana Bazo/Reuters; 28: FPG/Getty Images; 29 top: Stuart O'Sullivan/Getty Images; 29 bottom: Library of Congress; 30: The Washington Post/Getty Images; 31: Xinhua/Alamy Images; 32: Bloomberg/Getty Images; 34: Bloomberg/Getty Images; 35: Staff Sgt. Vernon Young Jr./US Air Force; 36: Bloomberg/Getty Images; 37: Nano Calvo/Alamy Images; 39: Darren Liccardo; 40: Mick Flynn/Alamy Images; 41: Juan Silva/Getty Images; 42: Jim Nicholson/Alamy Images; 43 top: Franck Fife/Getty Images; 43 bottom: Olivier Morin/Getty Images; 44: MixPix/Alamy Images; 45: Dave Kolpack/AP Images; 46: Polaris/Newscom; 48: Brandon Bailey/AP Images; 49: Amazon/REX Shutterstock/AP Images; 50 left: Jeff Chiu/AP Images; 50 right-51 bottom: Bloomberg/Getty Images; 51 top: ZUMA Press Inc/Alamy Images; 52: Daniel Zuchnik/Getty Images; 53: RosalreneBetancourt 7/Alamy Images; 54 top: Geo. R. Lawrence Co./Library of Congress; 54 bottom: Hans Adler/Wikimedia; 55 top: Arctic Images/Alamy Images; 55 bottom: Arctic Images/Alamy Images; 56: J.W.Alker/imageBROKER/Superstock, Inc.; 57: Ryan Brennecke/AP Images; 58: MIT; 59: Dave Kotinsky/Getty Images.

LIBRARY OF CONGRESS CATALOGING-IN-PUBLICATION DATA
Names: Otfinoski, Steven, author.
Title: Drones : science, technology, and engineering / by Steven Otfinoski.
Other titles: Calling all innovators.
Description: New York, NY : Children's Press, an imprint of Scholastic Inc.,
    [2017] | Series: Calling all innovators : a career for you | Includes
    bibliographical references and index.
Identifiers: LCCN 2016005330| ISBN 9780531218662 (library binding) | ISBN
    9780531219898 (pbk.)
Subjects: LCSH: Drone aircraft — Juvenile literature. |
    Aeronautics — Vocational guidance — Juvenile literature. | Remote
    sensing — Vocational guidance — Juvenile literature.
Classification: LCC UG1242.D7 O84 2017 | DDC 623.74/69023 — dc23
LC record available at http://lccn.loc.gov/2016005330

All rights reserved. Published in 2017 by Children's Press, an imprint of Scholastic Inc.
Printed in the United States of America 113

1 2 3 4 5 6 7 8 9 10 R 26 25 24 23 22 21 20 19 18 17

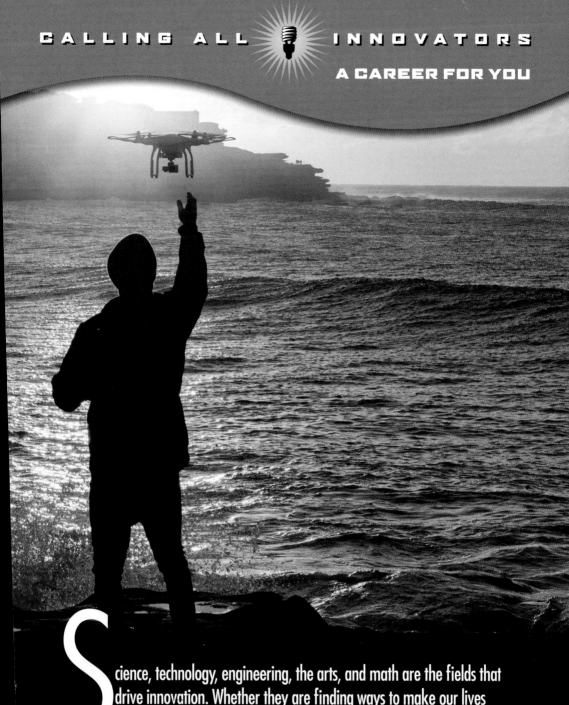

**S**cience, technology, engineering, the arts, and math are the fields that drive innovation. Whether they are finding ways to make our lives easier or developing the latest entertainment, the people who work in these fields are changing the world for the better. Do you have what it takes to join the ranks of today's greatest innovators? Read on to discover whether working with drones is a career for you.

# TABLE *of* CONTENTS

*Guided rockets used during World War II helped lead to modern drone technology.*

*Today, anyone can buy and operate a drone.*

*Many people work together to design and manufacture drones.*

AN INTERVIEW WITH

*Drones could soon become a common method of package delivery.*

An unmanned U.S. Navy helicopter prepares to land on a combat ship.

# CHAPTER ONE

# UNMANNED AIRCRAFT

F ew modern technological devices today have captured the world's imagination as much as unmanned **aerial** vehicles (UAVs). These pilotless aircraft are more commonly known as drones. They first came into major use as military weapons several decades ago. They took on an even larger role in recent years as part of U.S. military attacks on terrorists in the Middle East. However, drones are more than just weapons. They have also become useful tools for many other purposes, such as conducting scientific research, taking photographs, and just having fun. Controversial in both war and peace, these incredible aircraft are on the brink of becoming a significant force in nearly every aspect of modern life.

## THE DEVELOPMENT OF PROTO-DRONES

| 1849 | 1898 | 1917 | 1944 |
|------|------|------|------|
| The Austrian military drops bombs on its enemies from unmanned hot-air balloons. | The U.S. military takes photos of Spanish troops during the Spanish-American War using a kite camera. | The United States attempts to build unmanned "air torpedoes" during World War I. | Unmanned German V-1 rockets explode over Great Britain during World War II. |

## BALLOONS AND KITES

Even before airplanes conquered the sky, there were vehicles that flew without pilots. The Montgolfier brothers of France were the first to achieve flight using hot-air balloons. But before they sent animals and humans up in their balloons in 1783, the Montgolfiers tested unmanned balloons to see how they behaved.

Militaries soon saw the use of unmanned flying vehicles in war. In 1849, the Austrian military launched 200 pilotless balloons loaded with explosives toward Venice, Italy. During the American Civil War, both the Union and Confederate sides launched balloons behind enemy lines for **reconnaissance** and bombing. More than three decades later, during the Spanish-American War, the United States took aerial pictures of Spanish troops with a camera fixed to a kite.

*Frightened villagers gather to investigate after one of the Montgolfiers' unmanned balloons crashes in a town in France in 1783.*

## AIR TORPEDOES

The first manned airplanes were created in the early 1900s.

*Elmer Ambrose Sperry's designs helped lead to the creation of guided missiles.*

Almost immediately, militaries began using them to observe and attack enemies. But while air attacks were very effective, they also put pilots and other members of flight crews in harm's way.

When the United States entered World War I (1914–1918) in 1917, the U.S. Navy hired inventor Elmer Ambrose Sperry to help design "air torpedoes." These devices were basically airplanes loaded with dynamite. They could be launched into enemy territory using catapults. However, the project was a failure, with many of the planes crashing immediately after launching and others disappearing over the ocean. However, inventors and engineers did not give up on the idea of unmanned aircraft. In the 1930s, the U.S. Navy experimented with radio-controlled armored aircraft that were used as targets in bombing practice.

Remote controls were among the many innovations of inventor Nikola Tesla.

## TESLA'S TELEAUTOMATON

Inventor Nikola Tesla demonstrated one of the first wireless remotes in New York's Madison Square Garden in 1898. Tesla used his so-called teleautomaton to control the movements of a miniature boat. The device controlled the boat using **telegraph** signals. Tesla tried to sell his invention to the U.S. Navy, but they didn't think it would be practical for wartime use.

*This replica of Tesla's boat is on display near his birthplace in Croatia.*

**ANTENNAS RECEIVE RADIO SIGNALS FROM CONTROL DEVICE**

## IN CONTROL

Today, remote control devices are a common part of everyday life. You might use a remote to turn on your TV, play a video game, or fly a small drone in your backyard. But the ability to control a device from a distance was once a major technological breakthrough.

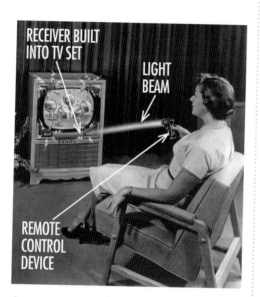

RECEIVER BUILT INTO TV SET

LIGHT BEAM

REMOTE CONTROL DEVICE

*A woman uses an early remote-control device in a 1955 ad for Zenith televisions.*

## TRICYCLES AND BOATS

In the early 1900s, Spanish engineer Leonardo Torres Quevedo invented his own telegraph transmitter similar to Tesla's. He called it the Telekino. Torres Quevedo used the device to guide a full-sized boat in the Spanish port of Bilbao. Later, he was also able to control a tricycle and submarine torpedoes.

## LIGHT VS. SOUND

By the 1930s, remote controls were being used to control radios and other electronic devices. They became especially popular for changing channels on TV sets. Early TV remotes emitted focused flashes of light. These signals were detected by a device built into the TV. Unfortunately, these devices couldn't always tell the remote's light apart from other sources, such as the sun or a lamp. They often changed the channel when the viewer didn't want them changed.

Later TV remotes used **ultrasound** signals instead of light. Ultrasound remotes were the standard until the 1980s, when **infrared**-light-signal remotes surpassed them. Unlike with earlier light-based remotes, infrared signals could easily be distinguished from other light sources. Today, many remotes use infrared-light signals. ☀

*Modern game controllers are a type of wireless remote.*

*A German V-1 falls over southern England in 1944.*

## WORLD WAR II

Military drones played a significant role in World War II (1939–1945). Germany invented the V-1, a small aircraft that carried a 1,900-pound (862-kilogram) explosive device. The V-1 was programmed to fly to its target and then plunge to the ground. The Germans launched 19,000 V-1s during the war, most of them at Great Britain. While the majority of them crashed or were shot down before reaching their targets, those that got through managed to injure or kill more than 20,000 people in Britain.

The U.S. Navy developed its own unmanned bombers as part of Operation Anvil. Remote control helped guide these explosive UAVs to their targets. However, they had to be flown part of the way to their destinations by pilots. The pilots were supposed to parachute out of the planes before they exploded on their targets. Unfortunately, many of the planes crashed early, and many pilots were killed.

## SLOW DEVELOPMENT

Following victory over Germany in World War II, the United States brought over the German scientists who had developed the V-1 to work in the budding U.S. space program. These experts created something similar to a drone with the guided cruise missile of the 1950s. Guided cruise missiles were part of the U.S. defense system in the Cold War against the Soviet Union. They were similar in many ways to the V-1. However, they were more likely to hit their targets.

During the Vietnam War (1954–1975), the United States dropped drones from airplanes to carry out reconnaissance missions. However, the drones could not return on their own. After their missions were complete, they had to be collected and brought back. The next step in drone development would be to create a UAV capable of flying to a location, completing a mission, and returning to base.

*A guided missile is launched from a U.S. Navy submarine in 1956.*

# FIRST THINGS FIRST

Leonardo da Vinci's helicopter design involved a single, spiral-shaped rotor.

## SPINNING THROUGH THE SKIES

Many present-day drones resemble tiny helicopters. Like full-sized helicopters, they rely on spinning blades called rotors to fly. The idea for a flying device based on this concept dates back hundreds of years. Kites that used spinning wings to fly may have been built as early as 400 CE in China. The inventor and artist Leonardo da Vinci sketched out an idea for a helicopter-like flying machine in the late 15th century. In 1784, two French inventors built a working toy helicopter that had a rotor made of bird feathers.

## SIKORSKY LEADS THE WAY

During the 19th century, numerous inventors tried unsuccessfully to create a full-sized helicopter that could get off the ground. In 1936, German inventor Heinrich Focke designed a twin-rotor helicopter that flew for more than an hour. However, it was very difficult to control.

It wasn't until 1939 that Russian American engineer Igor Sikorsky took to the air with the first practical helicopter, the VS-300.

Sikorsky's helicopter, like its more modern descendants, had many advantages over airplanes. It could take off and land vertically without a runway. Its

Heinrich Focke's twin-rotor helicopter is displayed at a 1938 event in Berlin, Germany.

MAIN ROTOR LIFTS
HELICOPTER INTO THE AIR

TAIL ROTOR CONTROLS
HELICOPTER'S DIRECTION

*Igor Sikorsky works the controls of his VS-300 helicopter.*

overhead whirling rotors allowed it to fly up, down, forward, backward, and even sideways. It could hover in one place for long periods. Soon, Sikorsky's company was producing helicopters for the U.S. military during World War II. The aircraft proved their worth in rescue missions, as they could travel places where planes couldn't go. They also were used for aerial observation and reconnaissance in enemy territory. During the Vietnam War, helicopters were used for combat.

# HELICOPTERS VS. DRONES

Many drones use the same type of overhead rotary blades as helicopters. However, they are much smaller and have no pilots. They have the same advantages in flight that helicopters do and are being used for some of the same work, such as aerial photography and rescue missions. Just as the helicopter outdid the airplane in many jobs, drones can reach places that larger helicopters can't get to. ✴

*U.S. soldiers travel aboard a UH-1D "Huey" helicopter during the Vietnam War.*

# DAY OF THE DRONE

On June 9, 1982, the drone became a true weapon of war. Israel, at war with Syria and Lebanon, launched its new Predator drones against Syria's antiaircraft missile defense sites. Israeli fighter planes used the drones to track down the location of the missile sites and destroy them.

The world took notice of this success. In the 1990s, the U.S. Air Force obtained Predator drones from Israel and used them to spy on enemy forces during the war in Kosovo. Then came the September 11, 2001, terrorist attacks on the World Trade Center in New York City and the Pentagon in Arlington, Virginia. The U.S. military sent drones to target the terrorist groups responsible for the attacks. The terrorists were operating out of Afghanistan and Pakistan, often in mountainous areas. The drones proved highly effective in hunting down enemies in difficult terrain where ground soldiers would have difficulty moving around.

## ABRAHAM KAREM

Inventor Abraham Karem is often called the father of the modern drone. Karem was a chief designer for the Israeli Air Force. He built his first important drone, the Albatross, in his garage using a modified go-kart engine. After that, he created the Predator. Karem later moved to the United States and established Karem Aircraft in Lake Forest, California. By 2013, the American military owned 8,000 of Karem's drones. They have been used for combat and **surveillance**.

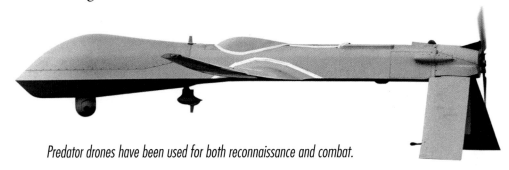

*Predator drones have been used for both reconnaissance and combat.*

*Afghan men examine the debris of a school destroyed by a U.S. drone attack.*

## PREDATOR ATTACKS

In February 2002, the first armed Predator was sent by the Central Intelligence Agency (CIA) to attack terrorist leader Osama bin Laden. Instead, it killed three innocent civilians. Though drones have now flown thousands of successful missions and killed hundreds of enemies, mistakes like this have made them highly controversial.

While drone technology has improved, there have continued to be accidents in which civilians have been killed. Many people question whether long-distance warfare is a good thing. Drone controllers are often thousands of miles away from combat, but they can push a button and kill an enemy they never see. While many enemy targets have been removed with little threat to U.S. military personnel, the victories often come with a heavy price. Many civilians are affected by these attacks. This only fuels the controversy surrounding drones.

FOUR ROTORS
LIFT DRONE

CAMERA

Most commercially available drones are small and highly maneuverable.

# CHAPTER TWO

# A SKY FULL OF DRONES

S ince the start of the 21st century, drones have moved from the world of war into peacetime uses. About 430,000 drones were sold in the United States in 2014. That number more than doubled in 2015. Most of these drones were purchased for recreational use. Others are used in such fields as agriculture, industry, police and rescue work, and science. On December 21, 2015, the Federal Aviation Administration (FAA) began requiring registration of drones weighing less than 55 pounds (25 kg). Earlier FAA regulations stated that drones couldn't fly above 400 feet (122 meters) and had to stay at least 5 miles (8 kilometers) from airports and sports arenas. With drones becoming so popular, many people felt that such laws were needed.

## DRONE FIRSTS

| 1983 | 1998 | 2001 | 2011 |
|---|---|---|---|
| The first High-**Altitude** Solar (HALSOL) drone takes to the skies. | An Australian drone is the first to fly across the Atlantic Ocean. | A drone is used as a weapon in Afghanistan for the first time. | On a North Dakota ranch, a drone is used to search for suspected criminals for the first time in the United States. |

*Police officers test a drone used to observe infrastructure and car crashes.*

# INDUSTRIAL DRONES

Today, the surveillance and information-gathering abilities of military drones are being applied to other fields with great success. For example, oil companies are using low-flying drones in Alaska to survey oilfields. Many of these oilfields are in remote areas that are difficult to reach. Drones help identify safe routes for workers to travel. They can also guide drivers along these roads when bad weather reduces visibility.

Some state departments of transportation are using drones to check the stability of bridges, highways, and other parts of local **infrastructure**. For example, in Minnesota, drones take high-definition photographs of bridges. These images are analyzed by engineers for potentially dangerous cracks and flaws that human inspectors could easily miss while viewing the bridges in person.

# ON THE FARM AND UNDER THE SEA

Drones are also helping with agricultural projects. For example, Indiana farmer Aaron Sheller set up drones with a live video feed so he could inspect his crops from a distance. It worked so well that Sheller started his own drone business. Precision Drone now serves farmers in 20 U.S. states and Canada. Since most farmland is unpopulated, the drones rarely interfere with human or animal life. The Environmental Protection Agency (EPA) has also used drones on federal farmlands to spray for insects, check for drought, and analyze soil.

In the Pacific Northwest, the U.S. National Oceanic and Atmospheric Administration (NOAA) uses a drone called an environmental sample processor to retrieve and analyze water samples. The information gathered by the drone helps NOAA monitor the health of shellfish.

*A Chinese farmer uses a drone to spread pesticides on crops.*

## BOTH SIDES OF THE LAW

Law enforcement agencies use drones to search for criminal suspects and escaped convicts. They have also used drones to strengthen surveillance at large public gatherings and other events where terrorism is a potential threat. Highway police use drones to monitor car accidents from the air and collect evidence to determine who is at fault.

Unfortunately, people on the other side of the law are beginning to use drones, too. Criminal groups have used UAVs to smuggle drugs and other illegal items into prisons. Other people are using drones to spy on their neighbors. Terrorists may try to use drones to spray toxic chemicals in the air over crowded public events.

*People can use drone-mounted cameras to take photos from far away.*

CAMERA

BOTTOM OF DRONE
MAKES LANDINGS
SMOOTH TO AVOID
DAMAGING CAMERA

*A lifeguard observes as a drone patrols a beach in California.*

## DRONES TO THE RESCUE

Because of their ability to reach remote locations that other aircraft can't, drones are ideal for search-and-rescue operations. They can get needed supplies to victims of floods, earthquakes, and other natural disasters. They can also report back to rescuers on precise locations of disaster victims, which helps speed up rescue efforts. Drones can even locate the wreckage of crashed airplanes or sunken ships.

Lifeguards on one beach in California are using drones to watch for sharks in the water. One New Jersey beach community is also studying the idea of using drones to bring life preservers to drowning swimmers. A drone could reach a drowning person much faster than a lifeguard could by swimming.

Drones can help animals as well as humans. In Africa, elephants and rhinoceroses are often the targets of **poachers**. Drones are being used to spot poachers in action. Nearby law enforcement officials can then find and stop them.

# MODERN MARVELS

*GPS technology is based on a network of 24 satellites.*

## GPS

The Global Positioning System (GPS) is a network of satellites that orbit Earth. Receivers on Earth can communicate with these satellites to pinpoint specific locations anywhere on the planet. Many people use GPS technology to navigate while driving or use maps on smartphones. Today, many drones are also equipped with GPS receivers. This helps them reach destinations around the globe.

*A geocaching enthusiast shows off the app she uses to search for treasure.*

*Thanks to GPS technology, people can find their way no matter where they are, unless obstructed by large structures or narrow canyons.*

## FROM MILITARY TO CIVILIAN USE

GPS was created in the 1960s to help the U.S. military protect the country from attacks. The military also used it to collect information about its enemies. Then, in 1983, the Soviet Union shot down a Korean passenger plane that had wandered into its airspace. U.S. president Ronald Reagan was concerned that such a tragic accident could happen to a civilian aircraft. To help pilots avoid potentially dangerous foreign airspace, GPS was opened up to civilian use.

## MORE APPLICATIONS

Today, GPS units are used for many different purposes by people all around the world. Scientists use GPS to study everything from climate change to earthquake patterns. GPS technology is also useful for making accurate maps. There is even a popular treasure-hunting game that relies on GPS. It is called geocaching. Participants use GPS to navigate to a given location. There, they look for a hidden container called a geocache. ✳

*A U.S. Geological Survey worker launches a drone used to observe bird populations.*

## DRONES IN SCIENCE

Scientists are using drones to explore and study the world around them. University naturalists have partnered with the U.S. Geological Survey Unmanned Aircraft Systems to use drones to survey the habitats of threatened wildlife species. Drones allow the scientists to get a close view of the animals' living conditions without disturbing them.

Drones not only aid threatened creatures but also help get rid of threatening ones. Scientists at the Virginia Military Institute have invented a land-traveling drone that emits carbon dioxide, mimicking human breath. Disease-carrying ticks are lured by the so-called tick rover, thinking they are following human victims. The dangerous pests are then killed. Other drones use one insect to fight another. An Australian agriculture student invented a flying drone that drops mites onto crops that are often damaged by the two-spotted spider mite. The dropped mites eat the spider mites and save the crops.

# AN ARCHAEOLOGICAL TOOL

Archaeologists use drones to explore the distant past. They can fly over ancient ruins to take photos of buildings and artifacts. For example, drones with heat-sensing cameras took pictures of an old Native American village buried under desert sands in New Mexico.

In Peru, archaeologists have flown drones over a mountain that is an ancient site of the 1,000-year-old Moche civilization. In just seven minutes, these drones can take detailed photographs of a section of the mountainside that would take three months for archaeologists to survey using traditional methods. The photographs are later turned into 3D images and detailed maps. These images have helped prove the existence of the ruins, preventing the site from being destroyed by building developers.

*An archaeologist surveys a site in Peru with the help of a drone.*

# FROM THIS TO THAT

*Boys show off their model airplanes in about 1925.*

## MODEL AVIATION

Today, many people enjoy flying small toy drones for fun. But long before toy drones took to the air, people built and flew small model airplanes. Like drones, these model planes are flown in public places by enthusiastic hobbyists using remote controls.

## A LONG HISTORY

Model airplane kits first gained popularity in the 1920s, after American pilot Charles Lindbergh's historic flight across the Atlantic Ocean. Over the next two decades, these model planes became lighter and faster thanks to the development of lightweight balsa wood and miniature gas engines. The American Academy of Model

Aeronautics (AAMA) was founded in 1936 to promote the interests of model aircraft users. Today the AMA ("American" has been dropped from the name) has about 170,000 members who belong to thousands of clubs and societies across the nation.

## MODEL PLANES VS. DRONES

Predating the FAA by more than two decades, the AMA has long had its own set of rules and regulations that members have followed. The AMA even helped the FAA develop the registration rules for unmanned aircraft. But the final regulations released in December 2015 have been controversial among model airplane fans. Many of these people feel that the FAA is trying to lump them together with drone users. "Everything that's remote control is a drone these days," complains Thomas Randall, president of a model aircraft society in Washington State. However, most model-airplane hobbyists are working out their differences with drone pilots and the FAA, and they aren't worried about the future of their hobby. "At the end of the day, when this all plays out, model aircraft are going to be pretty much the same as they ever were," says AMA official Rich Hanson. ✳

*Flying remote-controlled airplanes remains a popular hobby today.*

*A hobbyist launches his homemade model airplane at an event in 1941.*

# DELIVERY BY DRONE

One of the most potentially promising uses for drones is delivering consumer goods. In theory, almost anything that a human worker can deliver could be delivered faster and less expensively by a drone. This means drones could one day deliver everything from groceries to TVs.

In practice, drone delivery is still in the early stages. Technology companies such as Amazon and Google are testing drone delivery, with plans to be up and running by 2017. A textbook company in Australia is already making deliveries by drone, but in sparsely populated Australia there are fewer risks of drones interfering with people, animals, or airplanes. "Drone delivery is a difficult problem," admits American drone maker Chris Anderson. "They need to see their surroundings and avoid trees and birds and telephone lines and small children and dogs." The day may not be far off, however, when you order a pizza and it is delivered to your door not by a person in a car but by a flying drone.

*Some drones have been used to deliver medicine to remote, difficult-to-reach areas.*

*Regulations are intended to keep drone users from endangering others with their hobby.*

# RECREATIONAL DRONES

In recent years, the popularity of recreational drones has risen rapidly. As drone prices have dropped, sales have gone through the roof. People are buying drones in every shape and size. But this rise in popularity has also created problems.

Although new rules for registering drones are in effect, no training is required to fly a recreational drone. This has led to countless accidents and near misses. Drones have crashed in sporting events and on street corners. In October 2014, a drone hit power lines in West Hollywood, California, and knocked out power to hundreds of homes. More and stricter regulations will be needed as drones continue to gain popularity.

Workers perform tests on drones at a factory in Mexico.

# CHAPTER THREE

# ON THE JOB

**A**s drones become more popular among recreational users and are put to use for a variety of other purposes, the demand for new drone technology will grow rapidly. The Association for Unmanned Vehicle Systems International predicts that over the next decade, the drone industry will create more than 100,000 jobs and generate tens of billions of dollars in economic activity. Drones are on the brink of becoming one of the fastest growing industries in the world, and this growth is a golden opportunity for young people looking to enter the field. From engineers to **software** developers, skilled and experienced workers will be needed to keep the skies filled with drones.

## DRONES AND THE LAW

### 2012

The U.S. Senate passes a bill providing $63 billion to the FAA to stimulate the development of drones for government and commercial uses.

### 2014

A judge rules that a lack of laws dealing with drone use means that the FAA cannot fine anyone for using commercial drones.

### 2015

The FAA passes regulations requiring most recreational drones to be registered.

*Engineers make sure each individual part of a drone works correctly.*

## AEROSPACE ENGINEERS

Like other aircraft, drones are typically designed by aerospace engineers. These specialists begin a new project by determining what the drone will be used for. Will it be a small drone for people to fly in their backyards? Or will it be a high-speed military drone equipped with powerful weapons?

Once they know what they want their drone to do, engineers search for a way to achieve these goals. They find ways to fit all of the needed technology into a drone without making it too heavy or oddly shaped to fly. They also make sure that the design will operate in its intended environment. For example, a drone used to take photos inside a volcano needs to be able to endure intense heat. Others might need to be waterproof or withstand strong winds.

Once engineers have a design, they create a **prototype**. They use this early version of a drone to conduct tests and make improvements before creating a finished product.

## UAV OPERATORS AND PILOTS

Though drones are unmanned vehicles, most of them still require the skills of a pilot on the ground to fly successfully. Some drones can be controlled using a remote device that looks much like a video-game controller. However, professional drone pilots might also sit at a control center that looks much like the cockpit of a manned aircraft. They use control sticks, computer displays, and other controls to fly drones just as an airplane or helicopter pilot does. If a drone runs into trouble or becomes a threat to other aircraft or humans, its pilot must be able to land it quickly or, if necessary, crash it harmlessly. Large, complicated military drones may require a whole team to work with the pilot. This team could include mechanical technicians, sensor-systems controllers, and a commander who leads the mission or project.

SCREEN SHOWS IMPORTANT FLIGHT INFORMATION

CONTROLS USED TO OPERATE DRONE

*A member of the U.S. Air Force controls an MQ-9 Reaper drone from a base in Nevada.*

# SOFTWARE DEVELOPERS

Drones require a variety of software to operate correctly. Some might need navigation programs to help them locate their destinations. Others might use software to operate their cameras or communicate with a remote control device.

Software developers are the creative minds behind these programs. They start by determining which features a program needs. Then they figure out how all of these features can fit together without interfering with each other or making the program too complex. Once they have an idea in place, they work together with programmers to write the **code** that makes up the software. As they work, they might come across issues that need to be fixed. They might also come up with newer and better ideas as they work. Eventually, they create a finished version of the program.

*Developers and programmers work together to create drone software.*

*Some drones can be controlled using smartphone or tablet apps.*

## UPGRADES AND APPS

A software developer's job doesn't end once the first version of a program is completed. Once the software is released to a customer, developers may provide regular **upgrades** to keep the program current with new technology. They will also try to fix any bugs they might not have found while testing earlier versions of the software.

Government and military drones especially need regular upgrades. Military drones also need many supplemental programs. An aircraft's ground-control station may need hundreds of applications for such purposes as weather observation, tracking, and weapons release.

# AN INTERVIEW WITH DRONE ENGINEER DARREN LICCARDO

*Darren Liccardo is the vice president of engineering innovation for DJI, the world's leading manufacturer of consumer drones and creator of the best-selling quadcopter drone, Phantom 3. He works to improve core technology for the company's future products.*

**When did you first realize that you wanted to work with drones? Did any person or event inspire that career choice?** My grandfather was a pilot with United Airlines and taught me to build and fly model airplanes when I was a boy. I fell in love with flying and later in college got my pilot's license. As model planes changed and improved, I built and designed my own . . . I also developed a passion for cars. It was the dynamics and control of these vehicles that fascinated me.

**What kinds of classes did you take in school to prepare you for your career?** In middle school, I joined an after-school computer club run by my science teacher. These were still the early days of home computers, and it opened a new world to me. I fell in love with writing software code and seeing the results appear on the screen almost magically.

In high school, I focused on math and science. I went on to get a bachelor's and master's degree in electrical engineering and computer science at the University of California at Berkeley. It was a unique program that led me to focus on robotics and unmanned automated vehicles.

**What other projects and jobs did you do in school and your work life before beginning your career in drones?** Every summer I worked as a college intern, first at Lockheed Martin in aerospace technology and then at BMW, the car manufacturer. These summer jobs were really key to propelling me to a career in robotics and software. At the same time, I kept working on my own with model airplanes and created my own software and **hardware** to automate them. My first job after college was with a company that developed navigation systems for aerospace and robotics. I started there as a software engineer and gradually moved into leadership positions managing teams of engineers.

**How important is working in a team in your industry, and does working as part of a team come naturally to you?** Teamwork is critical in my business. There are so many complex components of drones and other robotic systems that just one person can't know it all. During my internships in college, I first learned how to be a team member and came to understand the importance of teamwork in creating a successful product in industry.

**What projects have you worked on that you're especially proud of?** I can think of two. I worked for BMW and Tesla on advancing the state of the art in automated driving, resulting in some really great products out in the wild now. On my own almost a decade ago now, I developed and flew a small automated electric delta-wing aircraft that flew continuously for two hours. That was a first.

**What would your dream drone look like, and what would it do?** My dream is to build a drone that can fly around the world on solar power. NASA built a drone called Helios that flew on solar power, but it was very large. I want to build a small drone that would resemble a large bird, like an albatross, with the advantages of biologically inspired aerodynamics and control.

**What advice would you give to a young person who wants to work with drone technology one day?** I would tell them to build and fly anything they can get their hands on—consumer drones, model airplanes, the latest hobby products, etc. Take courses in science and engineering in school to build a strong foundational knowledge in the relevant technology areas—everything is possible within the limitations of physics. Do as many internships as you can with technological companies in the field while in school. That early experience can be super valuable in shaping your path and interests. My internship at BMW in college later led me to a full-time job. Find your passion and don't settle for working on anything else. ☀

*Many videographers attach smartphones to their drone controllers so they can watch a live stream of the drone camera's video.*

## DRONE PHOTOGRAPHERS AND VIDEOGRAPHERS

Skilled photographers and videographers can expand their business by using drones. A new generation of lightweight aerial cameras with powerful, high-resolution lenses are producing photos and films that are in demand in a number of fields.

Freelance video **entrepreneurs**, known as vtreps, are hired by companies to capture video footage from their drones for a variety of purposes. Some create low-altitude aerial videos to help real estate agents sell homes and other properties. Resort and hotel owners are hiring videographers to create stunning marketing videos that bring in more guests. Conservation groups and environmental agencies employ videographers to track down poachers on film and gather evidence when businesses do not comply with conservation regulations.

## 3D MAPPERS AND MODELERS

A new generation of drones goes beyond capturing simple photos or videos. Some state-of-the-art drones are able to produce 3D models from the images they capture. Mappers and modelers can use this new technology in a number of areas. For example, technicians can scan a construction site and show the project's day-to-day progress as a computer-generated 3D model.

One company used drones to capture more than 6,200 images inside and outside of a 1,000-year-old Swiss castle over a four-hour period. The images were then converted into a 3D model of the castle. The Ground Truth Exploration group used drones to scan a mine in Yukon, Canada. They then highlighted "hot spots" on the model that showed the mining company where the richest veins of minerals were located. This enabled the mine to operate more efficiently.

*Drones can be used to monitor the progress of large construction projects.*

# THE ARTISTIC SIDE

*A film crew uses a drone to shoot a scene for the Indian film Shaandaar in 2014.*

## CAMERA! ACTION! DRONE!

Drones are transforming movies by allowing filmmakers to capture shots from incredible angles and positions that would otherwise be impossible. From mountain peaks to ground level, cameras mounted on drones are making movie and television action scenes more exciting than ever before. "Whenever you have a tool at your disposal that allows you to tell the story more efficiently and more poignantly, you use it," explains television producer Pieter Jan Brugge.

## SPORTS UP CLOSE AND PERSONAL

Drones are also being used to spice up the way television commercials, news programs, and televised sports events are filmed. Private individuals have disrupted football games and tennis matches with their unwelcome drones. Now coaches, athletes, and television producers are realizing that drones can be put to constructive use in sports. In the past, sports such as cycling and skiing could be difficult to film from exciting angles without

*Drones are a great way to get close-up footage at races.*

*A drone follows the action during a downhill skiing event.*

disrupting the athletes. Now, drones can fly around to capture video of these events from any angle. Drone footage is useful for more than just TV broadcasts. Coaches are using drones to record footage of games to study later with their players.

## DISNEY DRONES

In 2016, Disney theme parks climbed onto the drone bandwagon. Flying drones have become a part of the fireworks and lighting displays at both Disneyland and Disney World. Up to 50 drones are launched at once during these shows. Some of them work as floating movie screens, while others control flying puppet characters.

# TRAINING AND EDUCATION

Most people working in the drone industry have a bachelor's, master's, or even doctorate degree. Software developers often study such subjects as computer science, software engineering, or math. Those hoping to create drone hardware are likely to study some form of engineering. It takes more than just classroom learning to get a good job in the drone industry, though. Hands-on experience with drones of any kind will make a candidate stand out from the competition.

UAV operators and pilots need a UAV pilot certificate to get a job. One popular training program has three phases. The first is a Web-based ground school. The second allows the student to use a PC-based simulator. The third consists of hands-on flight training.

*Members of the U.S. Air Force listen as an instructor explains drone controls.*

*Students at the University of North Dakota use a flight simulator to practice flying drones.*

## A DEGREE IN DRONES

As of 2016, only a few colleges and universities offer an Unmanned Aircraft Systems degree. They include the University of North Dakota and Kansas State Polytechnic. One of the best and most comprehensive degree programs is at Embry-Riddle Aeronautical University's Daytona Beach Campus in Florida. The program started in 2011 with just 11 students and now has about 230. The curriculum includes the study of aerodynamics, remote sensing, and unmanned systems operations. Getting to fly drones around the campus for credit is every student's dream. "If I can do anything with UAVs, I will love to do it," says senior Jessica Brown, "whether that's being the actual pilot or just sensor operator, working the camera and stuff like that."

DRONE GRIPS
PACKAGE
SECURELY

*A prototype drone for Amazon's Prime Air service is displayed at a warehouse in 2015.*

# CHAPTER FOUR

# A DRONE'S JOURNEY

**B**ased on the success of Amazon's and other companies' drone delivery testing, drones may soon be bringing products of all kinds to our doorsteps. Amazon's Prime Air drone program could soon deliver up to 84 percent of the company's orders under 5 pounds (2.3 kg). By looking at drone delivery test programs and the challenges they have faced, we can imagine what a typical drone's journey from warehouse to your house might be like. Let's follow this new and exciting journey step-by-step from a drone's-eye view.

## LANDMARKS IN DRONE DELIVERY

| June 2013 | Dec. 2013 | Feb. 2015 | March 2015 |
|---|---|---|---|
| A Domino's Pizza restaurant in Great Britain releases video of its DomiCopter delivering pizza. | Amazon announces plans for its 30-minute drone delivery service, Prime Air. | Chinese e-commerce provider Ali Baba begins drone delivery service in several Chinese cities. | FPS, a distribution company, makes its first commercial delivery by drone in Sheffield, England. |

Workers at warehouses load items into bins so they can be packaged and shipped using drones or traditional methods.

## ORDER RECEIVED, DRONE DISPATCHED

The latest video game in your favorite series has just been released and you have to have it. You pick up your smartphone and place an order with a local store. The order is sent immediately to the company warehouse. An employee retrieves your packaged game from the warehouse's inventory. He or she deposits it into a small plastic bin and sends it down a roller track. At the rollers' end is a small "octocopter" drone that resembles a tiny helicopter. Its sensors tell it that the bin is beneath it, and its hooked legs attach themselves to the bin. The delivery drone can carry packages up to 5 pounds (2.3 kg) in weight. Your game is a lot lighter than that. The automated drone receives its orders via remote control and takes off out the open end of the warehouse.

# THE JOURNEY BEGINS

The drone runs on a battery that has a life of about 30 minutes. That means it can only deliver packages within a small **radius** of the warehouse. Luckily, your home is within that radius. The drone rises to a height of about 300 feet (91 m). This is high enough to avoid such obstacles as telephone and utility wires, but not so high that it will run into any airplanes. Still, the drone needs to watch out for other obstacles. In the sky, birds fly at a wide variety of altitudes. When the drone needs to land, there could be cars or people in the way. It uses sensors to avoid collisions. The drone also stays in communication with other drones flying in the area. They convey important information it needs for a safe flight, such as weather conditions, traffic flow, and landing conditions.

*Amazon's Prime Air drones weigh less than 55 pounds (25 kg), allowing them to easily reach high altitudes.*

Chris Anderson *wrote for magazines such as* Wired *and the* Economist *before founding 3D Robotics.*

## A GROWING BUSINESS

Anderson and Muñoz began their drone business in 2009 in Southern California. Muñoz became the chief technical officer and engineer, and Anderson is the chief executive and business manager. Since the company's founding, it has grown rapidly. In 2015, 3D Robotics had 180 employees and 30,000 customers around the world. It has recently expanded its manufacturing operation to China.

*Jordi Muñoz shows off a 3D Robotics prototype.*

## 3D ROBOTICS

3D Robotics is the largest manufacturer of commercial drones in the United States. Although it is a major force today, the company's beginnings were humble. In 2007, author and entrepreneur Chris Anderson made a drone at his dining room table to get his five children interested in science. He soon started a Web site for home drone enthusiasts called DIY Drones. Through the site, he befriended a young inventor named Jordi Muñoz, who was making his own drones at home.

*3D Robotics workers conduct tests on a drone.*

## THE SMARTEST DRONE

3D Robotics makes several models of drones at a wide range of price points. The company's most recent model is the Solo Drone. They claim that it is the smartest drone to date. It is powered by two computers and can take aerial photographs and video. Like other 3D Robotics drones, the Solo Drone is simple enough for a beginner to use but has enough features to interest a professional photographer. "Every time a new technology enables more choice, whether it's the VCR or the Internet, consumers clamor for it," Anderson has written. "Choice is simply what we want and, apparently, what we've always wanted." ✹

## IN THE AIR

The delivery drone has received information from another drone that the traffic ahead on the interstate highway is very heavy. While the drone is high enough to fly over the traffic, it could crash into moving cars if it had to suddenly land for any reason. To avoid this situation, the drone takes a detour and bypasses the interstate. It flies over open country and much less traveled roads. This adds only a few minutes to its airtime. But there is one challenge that the drone has not forseen. Drops of rain begin to fall. Drones do not normally fly in bad weather because **precipitation** can harm their sensors. But this is only a light shower, and soon the sun is out again, so the drone flies on.

*Delivery drones must be built to withstand a certain amount of bad weather.*

*Drones often capture attention from people on the ground as they fly overhead.*

## MAKING THE DESCENT

It's time for the drone to start its descent. It begins to drop down slowly. It reaches one hundred feet (30 m), then fifty feet (15 m). It is sailing over treetops and then a large field. A small herd of cows look up and moo loudly. The loud buzzing sound that drones make disturbs many animals.

The drone crosses a backyard where two boys are playing a game of catch. They stare up in awe at the drone as it flies overhead. Many people enjoy seeing a drone in the air. But not everyone. Some people complain about drones flying over their property. A few have actually fired guns at drones, trying to shoot them down. Other times, drones have had their cargo stolen or have been stolen themselves after landing.

# LASTING CONTRIBUTIONS

*Kite-mounted cameras provided a bird's-eye view of the damage in San Francisco after a major earthquake hit the city in 1906.*

## AERIAL PHOTOGRAPHY

Aerial photography is one of the primary uses of drones by both the military and private businesses. However, the idea of taking pictures from the sky goes back almost as far as the invention of photography itself. As early as 1860, photographers were taking pictures from hot-air balloons over cities and countrysides. By the 1880s, they were attaching their camera equipment to kites. In 1906, one photographer took pictures from kites of San Francisco after it was struck by a major earthquake. It took 17 kites to lift his heavy equipment to 2,000 feet (610 m). Three years earlier, European photographer Julius Neubronner mounted a tiny camera onto a carrier pigeon. The camera was set to take pictures automatically every 30 seconds while the bird was in flight.

*Julius Neubronner combined his interests in carrier pigeons and photography to take aerial photographs using birds.*

*Drones can be used to take photos of volcanoes and other dangerous areas.*

## PHOTOGRAPHING TWO WARS

Pilots in World War I spy planes took photographs behind enemy lines using reconnaissance cameras. By World War II, cameras were lighter and able to take clearer pictures from higher altitudes. By the war's end, scientists were sending rockets into Earth's orbit with cameras to take pictures of the planet and outer space.

*This beautiful overhead photograph of an Icelandic landscape was taken using a drone.*

## DRONE CAMERAS

In the past, aerial photography was generally limited to professionals who had the necessary equipment. But today, drones mounted with cameras have allowed even amateurs to take stunning pictures. More recently, even better cameras have evolved that are designed for use by professional photographers and filmmakers. These cameras feature larger sensors and interchangeable lenses, and they can take the highest-resolution photographs that have ever been taken. ✳

*A drone prepares to deliver a package in Germany.*

## DESTINATION IN SIGHT

The drone is approaching your house. The only problem is you aren't there. You decided to visit your friend who lives several blocks away. When you arrive, you notify the store on your smartphone that you are at a different location. The warehouse contacts the drone, and its GPS system quickly guides it to your new location. Sometimes, if home delivery is not convenient, a drone will deliver a package to a centralized drop-off location where you can pick it up later. But now you hear a whirring sound in the air. You look up from your friend's backyard. "There's my game!" you tell your friend. As you watch, the drone comes down for a perfect landing on your friend's lawn.

## MISSION ACCOMPLISHED

The drone's rotor blades stop spinning, and its hooked legs release the bin containing your game. Before you can reach it, the drone begins to ascend again. It is either being controlled by a remote operator back at the warehouse or working on its own automatic system. "Thanks, drone," you say, feeling a little foolish, as you watch it disappear from sight. Ten minutes later, it arrives back at the drone center, ready to be reloaded with another package and sent out for another delivery. While this drone's journey may still be in the future, that future may be closer than you think. Soon, you may be receiving everything from books to takeout food via drone. You may even have a drone of your own to fly. Happy landing!

*A boy shows off the quadcopter drone he used to film a large fire near his home.*

# THE FUTURE

GUIDE DRONE

*An experimental drone built at the Massachusetts Institute of Technology guides a student on a tour.*

## DRONES IN SPACE

In the future, drones may be flying higher than ever before. Technology giants Google and Facebook are developing high-altitude drone planes that can relay signals from satellites in space and beam down Internet service to remote parts of the planet that have never had Internet access before. Google predicts that its solar-powered drones will be able to remain in space for up to five years at a time.

## FOLLOW ME, PLEASE . . .

Another area back on Earth where drones may have a future is guided tours. The Massachusetts Institute of Technology is already testing a tiny drone that can take the place of student guides by leading visitors and prospective students on campus tours. It has a prerecorded speech and can get newcomers from one location to another with ease. The same technology may be used for tours of museums and historical sites.

# NEW CHALLENGES

There is still a lot of debate about how drones should be regulated. In the future, the government is likely to put more laws in place. These laws would be designed to prevent accidents and lawsuits. Here are some proposals for the future that have been discussed by citizens and lawmakers.

- Identify "drone zones" in cities and towns where residents can fly recreational drones without interfering with other aircraft, buildings, or people.

- Require users of large, heavy recreational drones to be trained in their operation and pass a test to become certified operators.

- Require manufacturers to develop new technology and devices that will prevent drones from operating in restricted areas or flying at altitudes above 400 feet (122 m). ☀

*Drones could become a common sight in the skies above towns and cities.*

# CAREER STATS

## SOFTWARE DEVELOPERS

MEDIAN ANNUAL SALARY (2015): $100,690

NUMBER OF JOBS (2014): 1,114,000

PROJECTED JOB GROWTH (2014–2024): 17%, much faster than average

PROJECTED INCREASE IN JOBS (2014–2024): 186,000

REQUIRED EDUCATION: At least a bachelor's degree

LICENSE/CERTIFICATION: None

## AEROSPACE ENGINEERS

MEDIAN ANNUAL SALARY (2015): $107,830

NUMBER OF JOBS (2014): 72,500

PROJECTED JOB GROWTH (2014–2024): −2%, a decline

PROJECTED INCREASE IN JOBS (2014–2024): −1,600

REQUIRED EDUCATION: At least a bachelor's degree

LICENSE/CERTIFICATION: None

## FILM AND VIDEO EDITORS AND CAMERA OPERATORS

MEDIAN ANNUAL SALARY (2015): $55,740

NUMBER OF JOBS (2014): 58,900

PROJECTED JOB GROWTH (2014–2024): 11%, faster than average

PROJECTED INCREASE IN JOBS (2014–2024): 6,400

REQUIRED EDUCATION: At least a bachelor's degree

LICENSE/CERTIFICATION: None

*Figures reported by the United States Bureau of Labor Statistics*

# RESOURCES

**BOOKS**

Collard, Sneed B. *Technology Forces: Drones and War Machines.* Vero Beach, FL: Rourke Education Media, 2013.

Dougherty, Martin J. *Drones: From Insect Spy Drones to Bomb Drones.* New York: Scholastic, 2014.

Marsico, Katie. *Drones.* New York: Children's Press, 2016.

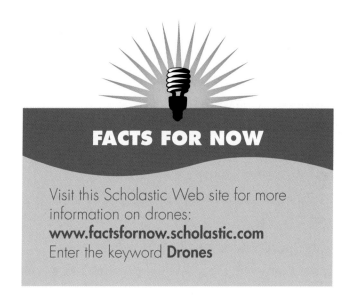

**FACTS FOR NOW**

Visit this Scholastic Web site for more information on drones:
**www.factsfornow.scholastic.com**
Enter the keyword **Drones**

# GLOSSARY

**aerial** (AIR-ee-uhl) having to do with flight

**altitude** (AL-ti-tood) the height of something above the ground or above sea level

**code** (KODE) instructions for a computer that are written in programming language

**entrepreneurs** (ahn-truh-pruh-NURZ) people who start and run their own businesses

**hardware** (HAHRD-wair) technological equipment

**infrared** (IN-fruh-red) a type of light that is undetectable by the human eye

**infrastructure** (IN-fruh-struhk-chur) roads, power grids, and other structures needed to support a community

**poachers** (POH-churz) people who hunt animals or plants illegally

**precipitation** (pri-sip-i-TAY-shuhn) rain, sleet, hail, or snow

**prototype** (PROH-tuh-type) the first version of an invention that tests an idea to see if it will work

**radius** (RAY-dee-uhs) an area measured as a circle around a central point

**reconnaissance** (rih-KAH-nuh-suhns) the act of observing an area to gain information about it

**software** (SAWFT-wair) computer programs that control the workings of the equipment, or hardware, and direct it to do specific tasks

**surveillance** (sur-VAY-luhns) close watch kept over someone or something

**telegraph** (TEL-i-graf) a device or system for sending messages over long distances using a code of electrical signals sent by wire or radio

**ultrasound** (UHL-truh-sound) sound that is too high for the human ear to hear

**upgrades** (UP-graydz) replacements of computer parts or software with better, more powerful, or more recently released versions

# INDEX

Page numbers in *italics* indicate illustrations.

# INDEX (CONTINUED)

# ABOUT THE AUTHOR

**STEVEN OTFINOSKI** has written more than 180 books for young readers, including books on the history of television, computers, and rockets. This is his sixth book in the Calling All Innovators series. He lives in Connecticut with his family.